# party nuts!

# party nuts!

50 recipes for spicy, sweet, savory, and simply sensational nuts that will be the hit of any gathering *by* sally sampson

THE HARVARD COMMON PRESS
BOSTON, MASSACHUSETTS

The Harvard Common Press
535 Albany Street
Boston, Massachusetts 02118
www.harvardcommonpress.com

Printed in China
Printed on acid-free paper

*Library of Congress Cataloging-in-Publication Data*
Sampson, Sally
   Party nuts! : 50 recipes for spicy, sweet, savory, and simply sensational nuts that will be
the hit of every gathering / Sally Sampson
     p. cm.
   ISBN 1-55832-243-4 (hc)
   1. Cookery (Nuts) I. Title
TX814 .S27 2002
641.6'45--dc21

2002024100

10   9   8   7   6   5   4   3

Interior and jacket design by Elizabeth Van Itallie
Photography by Duane Winfield
Food styling by Anthony Leberto
Prop styling by Duane Winfield and Justin Schwartz

Front jacket recipe: Paige's Hot Peppered Candied Walnuts, page 83
Back jacket recipes: (clockwise from upper left): Cumin-Cayenne Cashews, Pine Nuts, and
Pistachios, page 52; Slow-Roasted Southern Buttered Pecans, page 19; Jennifer Ligeti's
Classic Sugared Holiday Nuts, page 73; Hot Cayenne Tabasco Almonds, page 44

to the people who inhabit my nuthouse:
mark, lauren, benjamin, and tom

# acknowledgments

It really isn't possible to thank Carla Glasser or Jenny Alperen sufficiently for all that they contribute to my books and my life. Since this book was Carla's idea, it is actually true when I say that I couldn't have done it without her. Carla, may your life always be filled with MBs.

# contents

# introduction

**A**s soon as I decided to write this book, I sent an e-mail to all my friends: Do you have any recipes for party nuts—the edible, not the human, kind?

There is not a soul alive who would consider me a human party nut, and yet I have become so intrigued with the edible kind. The very thought of whipping up a batch makes me look forward to going to a party. So, does that mean that I am now a Party Nut? And the real question is: Is all this nuttiness now why people invite me?

It wouldn't surprise me. Party nuts are perfect for parties: sweet, salty, sometimes spicy, always rich, a little bit decadent, and yet one feels virtuous for eating them. In spite of the fact that nuts are high in fat, the fat is unsaturated (the good kind), they are totally lacking in cholesterol, and they are high in protein.

My fascination began a few years ago. Mark, my husband, invited his old college friend Scott MackIntosh for a visit. Scott's wife, Beverly, brought toys for Lauren and Benjamin, our two children, and a gift for me: a hand-tied bag of homemade roasted sweetened pecans. I won't say the rest is history . . . yet.

My first reaction was, I am loath to admit, pretty snobbish. Beverly's pecans seemed passé. But then I tasted them and literally didn't stop chomping until I had emptied the bag; I don't even recall offering any to Mark. I was wowed by Beverly's culinary prowess (never mind that she was also tall and beautiful) and stunned by how delicious and addictive the nuts were. In spite of the fact that I had written six cookbooks, it had never occurred to me to roast a nut of any kind.

I implored Beverly to give me her recipe. I replicated it exactly. But later, as one is wont to do in a pinch, I started to tinker with the ingredients, the temperature, and the timing. I bought a pound of pecans and later two and then, the following year, ten. I don't even have the original recipe anymore. I started to experiment with other nuts, different coatings, different methods, different temperatures. Eventually, there was almost nothing I wouldn't put on a nut. I explained it this way to my friend, cookbook writer and *Gourmet* magazine editor John Willoughby: I think of every possible flavor combination that would be good on one of many nuts and then try it.

Eventually, a friend suggested that I go into business, and in November of 2001 I decided to give it a try. I called my friends Olgo and Tony Russo, co-owners of A. Russo and Sons, a wholesale and retail produce market, and asked if they would try my Sweet and Spicy Pecans and, if they liked them, sell them. They loved them, but Olgo said they were a little too spicy, and Tony said they were not spicy enough. I knew then that I had reached a perfect ratio of sweet to spicy.

I asked Olgo how much he would need to sell to consider them a successful product. He said 30 pounds a month—but he ended up selling that much in the first week. I made batch after batch after batch in my small kitchen. I ordered extra sheet pans and, later, extra racks. I am not exaggerating when I say that my oven was on from the moment I woke up until the moment I went to sleep. The scent of sugar and spice pervaded the air, the furniture, even our clothing.

Mark, a sales and marketing vice president for start-ups and small companies, decided right then and there to quit his job. If A. Russo and Sons could sell 30 pounds in a week, he figured, this is a real business. We officially started Sampson's in 2002. Mark went on to open more and more accounts locally and then nationally. I can now say the rest is history.

a party
nut's
rule
book
*for*
making
party
nuts

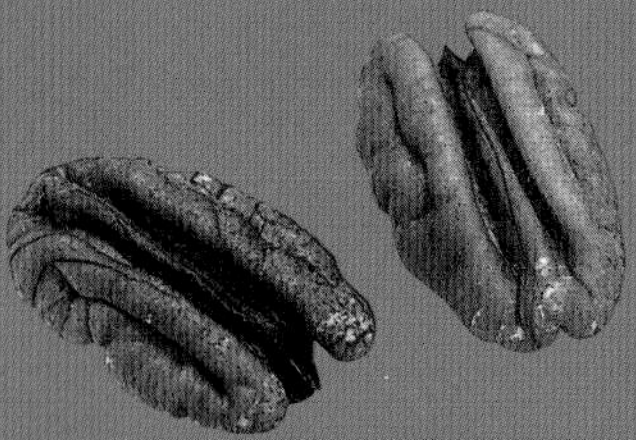

First of all, buy nuts from a reputable source that sells lots of nuts. Although they are sometimes more expensive, whole-food stores are good, as are wholesale clubs and Trader Joe's. I don't recommend little bags from grocery stores, as they tend to be old and have less taste.

Experiment with different kinds of nuts. I have discovered that subtlety is not something you generally find in a nut. Because of this, seasonings need to be strong to compensate for the dense richness of the nuts themselves. I usually prefer to use one type of nut per recipe, but nut mixes are also good. As a general rule, anything you can do with a pecan you can also do with a walnut, and anything you can do with an almond you can also do with a hazelnut. Beyond that, have some fun and monkey around with different varieties (and then be sure to send me a letter with the results).

I always store nuts in the freezer. While it won't hurt to refrigerate most nuts for up to three months, unless you are really sure about your source, you'll ensure against rancidity by freezing them. This goes for toasted, roasted, and sautéed nuts (including all the recipes in this book) as well as raw.

Even if you are eating nuts without adornment, you should always toast them first to intensify their flavor and their essential, well, nuttiness. You can cook them in a lower oven, say 250 degrees, but then you have to double or triple the cooking time. You can also cook them in a skillet, but I almost always burn them because, if you walk away, even for a second, it's a sure bet that that is the precise moment when they will be done. What follows is the most foolproof method for lightly toasted nuts.

Preheat the oven to 350°F. Place the raw nuts on a baking pan or sheet. It is not necessary to butter or oil it or to line it with parchment paper. If your oven heat is uneven, turn the nuts once or twice during the cooking time.

## TIME CHART OF LIGHTLY TOASTED NUTS

| Nut | Toasting Time |
| --- | --- |
| Almonds | 12 to 15 minutes |
| Hazelnuts | 12 to 15 minutes |
| Macadamias | 12 to 15 minutes |
| Peanuts | 15 to 20 minutes |
| Pecans | 10 to 12 minutes |
| Pine nuts | 10 to 12 minutes |
| Pistachios | 10 to 12 minutes |
| Walnuts | 10 to 12 minutes |

I have intentionally omitted roasting instructions for cashews. Although the cashew recipes in this book are roasted, when you are eating them simply salted, they are best prepared by cooking them in vast amounts of oil, which I don't think anyone wants to think about, never mind actually make. So if you enjoy munching on salted cashews, your best bet is to purchase them already roasted.

You must, absolutely must, completely cool nuts before storing them, whether you store them in a bag at room temperature or in the refrigerator or freezer. Otherwise, the residual heat in the nuts will create humidity in the container, the nuts will end up softening, and all your work will be for naught, because a party nut isn't a party nut if it isn't crisp. Unless specified, it is not necessary to cool nuts completely before eating them; this is simply a matter of taste.

Finally, remember that party nuts aren't just for parties: They're also great as a holiday or hostess gift. And there are lots of ways to package them. My favorite: in a cellophane bag tied with any kind of ribbon, including polar fleece strips, yarn, rope, hair ribbon, tulle, even fabric remains. Cellophane bags are available at paper and party stores in many colors and patterns (I like the clear). I also like to present party nuts in canning jars. Usually I make a square tag that my children decorate.

Here's my message in a nutshell. Have fun with these recipes. Play with different spices, different nuts, different combinations. Serve them in unusual containers at parties, like oversized martini glasses or Chinese food takeout containers, or on platters with olives and cheese. Give them as gifts, packed into candy dishes or muffin tins or coffee mugs. Keep them in your freezer for unexpected guests. Add them to salads, ice cream, oatmeal, sandwiches, dips, soups, and stews. Go wherever your imagination and your palate take you.

# savory
## nuts

- shellacked balsamic pecans
- curried pecans with orange
- slow-roasted southern buttered pecans
- pistachios with anise
- saffron pistachios
- spiced macadamia nuts
- greek pistachios and pine nuts
- curried coriander spiced pistachios
- pesto pine nuts
- indian almonds with coconut
- garlic almonds and hazelnuts
- chris and doc's zaatar almonds and pistachios
- curried garlic peanuts
- rosemary walnuts
- soy-glazed walnuts

# shellacked balsamic pecans

I had six friends over for a nut fest and swore that no one would be able to guess the flavorings of this unusual pecan, and yet my friend Toni Bowerman did just that. In fact, in a group of about twelve contenders, these were her hands-down favorite. In spite of all the sugar, these are not very sweet; rather, the balsamic vinegar gives them an appealing sourness.

2 cups lightly toasted pecan halves (page 12)
½ cup firmly packed brown sugar
⅓ cup balsamic vinegar
½ teaspoon kosher salt
¼ teaspoon chili powder or cayenne pepper (optional)

1. Line a baking sheet with parchment paper.
2. Place the pecans, brown sugar, and vinegar in a large, heavy-bottomed skillet and cook over medium heat, stirring, until the sugar melts, the pecans are well coated with the mixture, and there is no liquid at the bottom, 3 to 5 minutes. Sprinkle evenly with the salt and chili powder, if using.
3. Transfer the pecans to the prepared sheet, separating the individual nuts. Set aside to cool before serving.

MAKES 2 CUPS

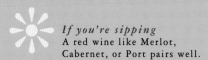

*If you're sipping*
A red wine like Merlot, Cabernet, or Port pairs well.

*Not just for snacking*
Swirl them into vanilla ice cream and/or with strawberries drizzled with additional balsamic vinegar.

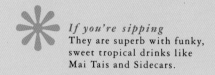

*If you're sipping*
They are superb with funky,
sweet tropical drinks like
Mai Tais and Sidecars.

*Not just for snacking*
Try these atop a bowl of
butternut squash soup.

# curried pecans with orange

The sweetness of the orange juice contrasts nicely with the slightly biting flavor of the curry, which in turn plays up the natural sweetness of the pecans. These are excellent when made with walnuts but just slightly sweeter and milder with pecans.

Don't substitute prepared orange juice for the concentrate, which is stickier and stronger. Mango, pineapple, or orange sorbet makes a better substitute.

1 large egg white (2 tablespoons)
1 tablespoon frozen orange juice concentrate
2 to 3 teaspoons curry powder, to taste
1 teaspoon kosher salt
¼ to ½ teaspoon cayenne pepper (optional), to taste
2 cups raw pecan halves
¼ cup sugar
Grated zest of 1 orange

1. Preheat the oven to 225°F. Line a baking sheet with parchment paper.

2. Place the egg white in a large stainless steel bowl and whip until frothy. Whip in orange juice concentrate, curry powder, salt, and, if desired, cayenne. Add the pecans and toss until completely coated. Add the sugar and toss again.

3. Transfer the nuts to the prepared sheet and arrange in a single layer. Place in the oven and cook, stirring every 15 minutes, until lightly colored and dried out, about 1 hour and 15 minutes.

4. Remove from the oven, immediately loosen the nuts with a metal spatula, sprinkle with the orange zest, and set aside to cool before serving.

MAKES 2 CUPS

# slow-roasted southern buttered pecans

**A** simple, traditional, age-old recipe, these nuts are best served with semi-soft cheeses, such as Hubbardston blue goat cheese or Saint-Nectaire, and crisp pears or apples, like Macouns, my favorite.

4 cups raw pecan halves
2 tablespoons unsalted butter, cut into pieces
Kosher salt to taste

1. Preheat the oven to 250°F. Line a baking sheet with parchment paper.
2. Place the pecans on the prepared sheet and arrange in a single layer. Place in the oven and roast, stirring every 15 minutes, until they turn a deep brown color, about 1 hour.
3. Remove from the oven, immediately loosen the nuts with a metal spatula, add the butter, and stir until the nuts are well coated. Sprinkle evenly with salt and serve immediately or set aside to cool.

MAKES 4 CUPS

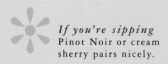

*If you're sipping* Pinot Noir or cream sherry pairs nicely.

# pistachios
## with anise

It's no surprise that I have become obsessed with nuts. When our family recently went out for ice cream at Toscanini's Ice Cream, in Cambridge, I spied a new and unfamiliar flavor: pistachio anise. I tasted it (though I had a scoop of burnt sugar ice cream instead) and immediately ran home to try this combination on nuts.

The pistachio, also known as the green almond, originated in Persia. The most common use for pistachios, not surprisingly, is pistachio ice cream, which was invented by Philadelphia's James W. Parkinson in the 1940s.

2 cups shelled raw pistachio nuts
2 teaspoons vegetable oil
1½ tablespoons Sambuca or any anise-flavored liqueur
1 teaspoon kosher salt
1 teaspoon anise seeds

1. Place all the ingredients in a large, heavy-bottomed skillet and cook over high heat, stirring, until the liquid is absorbed, 2 to 3 minutes.

2. Reduce the heat to low and cook, stirring occasionally, until the nuts have darkened, about 10 minutes. Transfer the nuts to a plate and set aside to cool before serving.

MAKES 2 CUPS

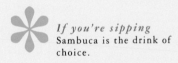

*If you're sipping*
Sambuca is the drink of choice.

*Not just for snacking*
Tipping my hat to the original inspiration, mix them into vanilla ice cream.

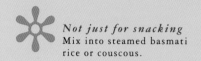

*Not just for snacking*
Mix into steamed basmati
rice or couscous.

# saffron pistachios

**V**ery subtle, with an almost delicate saffron flavor that improves
over time, these nuts really need to cool completely before serving.
If you haven't had a good pistachio lately, it's probably
because you're eating those grown in California. Although they're easier to
open and comparatively large, their flavor isn't as good as the smaller,
more flavorful Turkish pistachios.

Saffron, the world's most expensive spice, is fortunately so flavorful that
you need only a tiny bit to flavor foods. Used most famously in risotto
Milanese, paella, and bouillabaisse, saffron adds a kind of aromatic pun-
gency and a gorgeous yellow color.

> 2 cups lightly toasted shelled pistachio nuts (page 12)
> 2 tablespoons olive oil
> 4 saffron threads, crushed, or 1 teaspoon curry powder
> ½ teaspoon kosher salt

1. Preheat the oven to 250°F. Line a baking sheet with parchment paper.
2. Place the pistachios and oil in a medium-size bowl and toss to combine. Add the saffron and salt and toss until the nuts are well coated.
3. Transfer the pistachios to the prepared sheet and arrange in a single
layer. Place in the oven and cook until the nuts just begin to color, about
20 minutes.
4. Remove from the oven, transfer the nuts to a paper towel to drain,
and set aside to cool before serving.

MAKES 2 CUPS

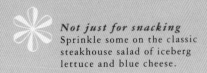

*Not just for snacking*
Sprinkle some on the classic
steakhouse salad of iceberg
lettuce and blue cheese.

# spiced
# macadamia nuts

**R**ich, creamy, crunchy, and spicy, this rendition made a convert out of me. I can't say I ever cared for macadamia nuts until I tried these.

1 tablespoon vegetable oil
2 cups raw macadamia nuts
1 heaping tablespoon sugar
1 teaspoon curry powder
1 teaspoon ground cumin
1 teaspoon ground coriander
1 teaspoon chili powder
1 teaspoon kosher salt
½ teaspoon cayenne pepper, or more to taste

1. Preheat the oven to 250°F. Line a baking sheet with parchment paper.
2. Place the oil and nuts in a medium-size bowl and toss until well coated. Add the remaining ingredients and mix well to coat evenly.
3. Transfer the nuts to the prepared sheet and arrange in a single layer. Place in the oven and bake until lightly browned, stirring occasionally, 25 to 30 minutes.
4. Remove from the oven, immediately loosen the nuts with a metal spatula, and set aside to cool before serving.

MAKES 2 CUPS

# greek pistachios and pine nuts

**T**he ingredients in these nuts, as well as the nuts themselves, are customarily found in many Greek dishes. They are best paired with a big hunk of feta cheese, marinated olives, and figs (either fresh or dried will do).

1 cup lightly toasted shelled pistachio nuts (page 12)
1 cup lightly toasted pine nuts (page 12)
2 teaspoons olive oil
¾ teaspoon dried Greek oregano
1 teaspoon chopped fennel seeds
½ teaspoon kosher salt
½ teaspoon freshly ground black pepper
Grated zest of ½ lemon

1. Preheat the oven to 300°F. Line a baking sheet with parchment paper.

2. Place the nuts and oil in a large bowl and toss until well coated. Add the oregano, fennel seeds, salt, and pepper and toss again to coat evenly.

3. Transfer the nuts to the prepared sheet and arrange in a single layer. Place in the oven and cook until they begin to color, about 10 minutes.

4. Remove from the oven, immediately loosen the nuts with a metal spatula, sprinkle evenly with the lemon zest, and set aside to cool before serving.

MAKES 2 CUPS

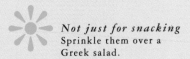

*Not just for snacking*
Sprinkle them over a
Greek salad.

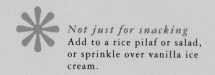

*Not just for snacking*
Add to a rice pilaf or salad,
or sprinkle over vanilla ice
cream.

# curried coriander spiced pistachios

They are crunchy, delicate, and spicy, but not hot.
Although they come from the same plant, coriander (the seed)
and cilantro (the leaf) are neither interchangeable nor even
remotely similar in taste. The seeds, used here and primarily in pickling,
have a slightly lemony sage flavor.

2 cups lightly toasted shelled pistachio nuts (page 12)
1 tablespoon olive or vegetable oil
2 tablespoons sugar
1½ teaspoons kosher salt
1 tablespoon plus 1 teaspoon curry powder
2 teaspoons ground coriander
½ teaspoon ground cumin
½ teaspoon ground cinnamon

1. Place all the ingredients in a large, heavy-bottomed skillet over low
heat and cook, tossing, until the sugar melts and the nuts are well coated,
4 to 5 minutes.

2. Remove from the heat, transfer the nuts to a large plate in a single
layer, and set aside to cool before serving.

**MAKES 2 CUPS**

# pesto pine nuts

Very expensive and delicately flavored, pine nuts are also called *pignoli* and *piñons*. They are harvested from pine trees and can be found inside the pine cone, a fact that I came to realize only after betting that they didn't. Most of the pine nuts Americans use are the thin, subtler Italian variety, but a stronger variety is available in Asian markets.

2 cups lightly toasted pine nuts (page 12)
3 tablespoons store-bought or homemade pesto
1 tablespoon finely grated parmesan cheese
1 teaspoon kosher salt

1. Place all the ingredients in a large bowl and toss to combine.
2. Transfer the nuts to a large plate in a single layer and set aside to dry for at least 2 hours.

MAKES 2 CUPS

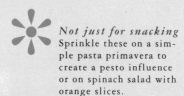

*Not just for snacking*
Sprinkle these on a simple pasta primavera to create a pesto influence or on spinach salad with orange slices.

# indian almonds with coconut

T he babysitter arrives, we choose a late movie, and then begin the night at one of our favorite East Indian restaurants in Waltham, Massachusetts. The meals are exotic, the spices aromatic, and the rice pudding—suffused with rose water and cardamom—is sprinkled with a version of these spicy almonds. It's a heady and rich combination that stays with me even after the babysitter goes home.

1 teaspoon curry powder
1 teaspoon chili powder
¼ teaspoon garlic powder
¼ teaspoon ground ginger
¼ teaspoon ground cardamom
2 tablespoons flaked coconut, sweetened or unsweetened
1 tablespoon canola or olive oil
2 cups raw whole almonds, blanched or skin on
1 teaspoon kosher salt
Grated zest of 1 lime

1. Preheat the oven to 250°F. Line a baking sheet with parchment paper.
2. Place the curry powder, chili powder, garlic powder, ginger, cardamom, coconut, and oil in a medium-size bowl and toss to combine. Add the almonds and mix.
3. Transfer the nuts to the prepared sheet and arrange in a single layer. Place in the oven and cook, stirring every 15 minutes, until lightly colored, about 45 minutes.
4. Remove from the oven, immediately loosen the nuts with a metal spatula, sprinkle evenly with the salt and lime zest, and set aside to cool before serving.

MAKES 2 CUPS

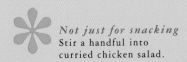

*Not just for snacking*
Stir a handful into
curried chicken salad.

*Not just for snacking*
They are a great addition
when chopped and sprinkled
over steamed or sautéed dark
leafy vegetables such as broc-
coli rabe, spinach, or kale.

# garlic almonds and hazelnuts

california is the only state that produces almonds commercially. Seventy percent of the world's supply is grown by 6,000 farmers on almost half a million acres. Almonds are not actually nuts, botanically speaking, but are the seeds of stone fruits, like the pit of a peach. They are rich in protein, calcium, and riboflavin. Only a small portion of the fat in almonds is saturated, and the almond's fat content is among the lowest of the nuts.

Pine nuts are also great cooked this way. Keep your eye on these to be sure the garlic doesn't burn.

2 cups raw whole almonds or hazelnuts, or a combination, skin on
1 tablespoon olive oil
2 teaspoons finely minced garlic
½ teaspoon garlic powder

1. Preheat the oven to 250°F. Line a baking sheet with parchment paper.
2. Place all the ingredients in a medium-size bowl and toss until the nuts are well coated.
3. Transfer to the prepared sheet and arrange in a single layer. Place in the oven and cook until the nuts begin to color, about 20 minutes.
4. Transfer to a paper towel to drain and set aside to cool before serving.

MAKES 2 CUPS

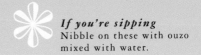

*If you're sipping*
Nibble on these with ouzo
mixed with water.

# chris and doc's zaatar almonds and pistachios

I was looking through Chris Schlesinger and John Willoughby's book *Big Flavors of the Hot Sun* for inspiration and read a recipe too quickly, thinking that Grilled Chicken Thighs with Persian-Style Nut Rub was for chicken with spiced nuts. It wasn't, but I had already gotten excited about the possibilities and ended up creating this spiced nut mix.

Zaatar can be found in most ethnic markets that have an extensive spice selection. Made up of sesame seeds, sumac, and thyme, it is popular in the Middle East, where it is sprinkled on salads, vegetables, meats, and breads. Sumac, the berry of a bush that is considered solely decorative in the West, gives the mixture a kind of fruity but slightly sour taste. I call for Greek oregano because I prefer it to all others. To toast the sesame seeds, just add them to the almonds and pistachios during the last five minutes of their initial toasting.

1 cup lightly toasted whole almonds (page 12), blanched or skin on
1 cup lightly toasted shelled pistachio nuts (page 12)
1 tablespoon vegetable oil
2 tablespoons toasted sesame seeds (see headnote)
½ to 1 teaspoon kosher salt, to taste
1 teaspoon dried Greek oregano
1 teaspoon zaatar
Pinch of cayenne or freshly ground black pepper

Place everything in a medium-size bowl and toss to combine and coat evenly. Set aside to cool completely before serving.

MAKES 2 CUPS

# curried garlic peanuts

**P**eanuts, also known as monkeynuts or groundnuts, are not actually nuts but are really legumes (plants that have seed pods that split along both sides) that grow underground. It's best not to include them in mixes unless you are certain that none of your guests is allergic.

2 cups lightly toasted shelled peanuts (page 12)
1 teaspoon peanut or olive oil
1 teaspoon garlic powder
1 teaspoon curry powder
1½ teaspoons kosher salt

1. Preheat the oven to 250°F. Line a baking sheet with parchment paper.

2. Place the peanuts, oil, garlic powder, and curry powder in a medium-size bowl and toss until the nuts are well coated.

3. Transfer the nuts to the prepared sheet and arrange in a single layer. Place in the oven and bake for 10 minutes.

4. Remove from the oven, sprinkle evenly with the salt, immediately loosen the nuts with a metal spatula, and set aside to cool for 1 hour before serving.

**MAKES 2 CUPS**

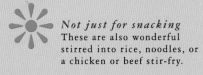

*Not just for snacking*
These are also wonderful stirred into rice, noodles, or a chicken or beef stir-fry.

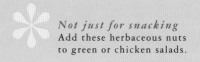

*Not just for snacking*
Add these herbaceous nuts
to green or chicken salads.

# rosemary walnuts

You can make these savory cocktail nuts with almost any kind of nut—cashews, pecans, and peanuts are good choices—and almost any herb—oregano, thyme, and tarragon work well.

Look for walnuts that are pale in color. Although rich and flavorful, walnuts are bitter to some people. If you feel this way, simply remove the skins by rubbing the nuts with a towel after toasting them, before you add any other ingredients.

2 cups lightly toasted walnut halves (page 12)
1 tablespoon vegetable or walnut oil
1 tablespoon unsalted butter, melted
2 tablespoons chopped fresh rosemary leaves or 2 teaspoons dried
½ teaspoon ground sage
1 teaspoon sweet paprika
1 teaspoon kosher salt
½ teaspoon cayenne pepper (optional)

1. Preheat the oven to 300°F. Line a baking sheet with parchment paper.

2. Place all the ingredients in a large bowl and toss until the nuts are well coated.

3. Transfer the nuts to the prepared sheet and arrange in a single layer. Place in the oven and bake, stirring every 10 minutes, until the nuts are fragrant and deeply colored, 20 to 30 minutes.

4. Remove from the oven, immediately loosen the nuts with a metal spatula, and set aside to cool before serving.

MAKES 2 CUPS

# soy-glazed walnuts

**U**nlike the ubiquitous tamari almond, these are glazed, not dusted, and have a great brittle-like, salty crunch. And they are versatile: They are just as delicious sprinkled over vanilla ice cream as they are incorporated into savory Asian dishes.

2 cups raw walnut halves
¼ cup soy sauce
1 tablespoon unsalted butter, melted
2 tablespoons sugar

1. Preheat the oven to 225°F. Line a baking sheet with parchment paper.

2. Place all the ingredients in a large bowl and toss until the nuts are well coated.

3. Transfer the nuts to the prepared sheet and arrange in a single layer. Place in the oven and cook, stirring occasionally, until golden, 30 to 35 minutes.

4. Remove from the oven, immediately loosen the nuts with a metal spatula, and set aside to cool before serving.

**MAKES 2 CUPS**

*If you're sipping*
Serve with an Asian lager-type beer.

# hot
# nuts

cumin-chili pecans

cajun pecans

roasted southern pecans sweet and piquant

pecans au poivre

coriander-chili almonds

hot cayenne tabasco almonds

bbq pecans

toasted cumin hot pecans

hot pepper sesame peanuts

salt and chipotle chile almonds

three-pepper almonds

cumin-cayenne cashews, pine nuts, and pistachios

killer peanuts

smoky spicy peanuts

curried chili cashews

roasted tabasco pecans

texas chili–inspired spicy pecans

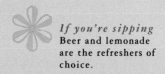

*If you're sipping*
Beer and lemonade
are the refreshers of
choice.

# cumin-chili pecans

**A**n almost sweet, subtly spicy before-dinner snack, these savory pecans are fantastic accompanied by guacamole, taquitos, and almost anything fried. The cumin flavor, though not overwhelming, predominates.

1 large egg white (2 tablespoons)
½ teaspoon ground cumin
½ teaspoon chili powder
¼ teaspoon ground ginger
¼ teaspoon ground cinnamon
¼ teaspoon cayenne pepper
1 teaspoon kosher salt
2 cups raw pecan halves
2 tablespoons sugar

1. Preheat the oven to 225°F. Line a baking sheet with parchment paper.

2. Place the egg white in a large stainless steel bowl and whip until frothy. Add the spices and salt and mix to combine. Add the pecans and toss until completely coated. Add the sugar and toss again.

3. Transfer the nuts to the prepared sheet and arrange in a single layer. Place in the oven and cook, stirring every 15 minutes, until lightly colored and dried out, about 1 hour and 15 minutes.

4. Remove from the oven, immediately loosen the nuts with a metal spatula, and set aside to cool before serving.

MAKES 2 CUPS

# cajun pecans

The McIlhenny Company, maker of Tabasco sauce since the mid-1800s, recently expanded its line of fiery pepper sauces. Don't feel you have to stick with the traditional red sauce; instead, try chipotle, green, habanero, or garlic pepper.

2 cups lightly toasted pecan halves (page 12)
1 tablespoon Worcestershire sauce
½ teaspoon Tabasco sauce
¾ teaspoon ground cumin
½ teaspoon sweet paprika
½ teaspoon garlic powder
2 teaspoons kosher salt

1. Preheat the oven to 325°F. Line a baking sheet with parchment paper.

2. Place all the ingredients in a large bowl and toss until the pecans are completely coated with the mixture.

3. Transfer the nuts to the prepared sheet and arrange the pecans in a single layer. Place in the oven and cook, stirring often, until lightly colored and dried out, about 15 minutes.

4. Remove from the oven, immediately loosen the nuts with a metal spatula, and set aside to cool before serving.

MAKES 2 CUPS

*If you're sipping*
Cool these spicy morsels down with beer, white wine, or a Cajun martini (for the martini, ask at your local liquor store for pepper-infused vodka).

*Not just for snacking*
Try sprinkling these over rice or mixing them into stuffing.

*If you're sipping*
Serve with iced tea or
lemonade.

*Not just for snacking*
Try mixing broken pieces
into cornbread for a spicy,
crunchy sensation.

# roasted southern pecans sweet and piquant

Look out: These are addictive! For a hotter and even more pungent dish, go with the larger amount of cayenne. Watch these carefully—Worcestershire burns easily.

1 large egg white (2 tablespoons)
½ cup sugar
2 tablespoons sweet paprika
2 teaspoons Worcestershire sauce
1 to 2 teaspoons cayenne pepper, to taste
½ teaspoon kosher salt
2 cups raw pecan halves

1. Preheat the oven to 250°F. Line a baking sheet with parchment paper.

2. Place the egg white in a large stainless steel bowl and whisk until frothy. Whisk in the sugar, paprika, Worcestershire, cayenne, and salt. Add the pecans and toss until completely coated.

3. Transfer the pecans to the prepared sheet and arrange in a single layer. Place in the oven and cook, stirring every 15 minutes, until lightly colored and dried out, about 1 hour and 15 minutes.

4. Remove from the oven, immediately loosen the nuts with a metal spatula, and set aside to cool before serving.

MAKES 2 CUPS

*Not just for snacking*
These are wonderful
sprinkled over grilled
steak (add some crumbled
blue cheese, too) or
tossed into fettuccine
Alfredo or mashed pota-
toes with sour cream.

# pecans au poivre

For pepper lovers only, these nuts can definitely cause an addic-
tion. The technique of cooking them first in a melted mixture of
salt, sugar, and pepper creates a hard coating. This coating is then
covered in the same mixture, but not cooked again, which results in a
pecan with a sort of attractive, but weird, gray dusting. Don't grind the
pepper too fine—keep it coarse.

For great contrast, serve these with a triple-cream cheese such as
Explorateur.

**2 tablespoons kosher salt**
**¼ cup coarsely ground black pepper**
**½ cup sugar**
**2 cups lightly toasted pecan halves (page 12)**

1. Place the salt, pepper, and sugar in a medium-size bowl and toss to
combine.

2. Place a large, heavy-bottomed skillet over high heat and, when it is
hot, add the pecans and two thirds of the sugar mixture and cook, stirring
occasionally, until the sugar has melted and completely coats the pecans.

3. Remove from the heat, add the remaining sugar mixture, and toss
until well dusted. Transfer the nuts to a large plate and set aside to cool
before serving.

**MAKES 2 CUPS**

# coriander-chili
# almonds

**T**he great strong flavors in these nuts benefit from sitting out to dry for a few hours and up to overnight. But don't wait too long: The spices will fall off after a day or two.

This preparation also works well with pine nuts, pistachios, macadamias, and hazelnuts.

2 cups lightly toasted whole almonds (page 12), blanched or
  skin on
2 teaspoons vegetable oil
2 teaspoons ground coriander
2 teaspoons ground cumin
2 to 3 teaspoons chili powder, to taste
1½ to 2 teaspoons kosher salt, to taste
¼ to ½ teaspoon cayenne pepper (optional), to taste

1. Preheat the oven to 300°F. Line a baking sheet with parchment paper.

2. Place all the ingredients in a medium-size bowl and toss to combine.

3. Transfer the nuts to the prepared sheet and arrange in a single layer. Place in the oven and cook for 5 minutes.

4. Remove from the oven and set aside to dry for at least 4 hours before serving.

**MAKES 2 CUPS**

✱ *Not just for snacking*
Add these to green or chicken salads, or to an Indian rice dish such as biryani.

# hot cayenne
# tabasco almonds

The heat from these fiery nuts doesn't hit right away. It shows up just when you have finished the nut, which makes you want more. And then it happens again. And again. Yes, they are addictive. Dry mustard, also called powdered mustard, should really be called ground mustard seed. It seems as if it should be dehydrated prepared mustard, but in fact you use dry mustard to make prepared mustard. It's sort of backward.

2 cups raw whole almonds, blanched or skin on
2 tablespoons unsalted butter, melted
2 tablespoons Tabasco sauce (any variety)
2 teaspoons Worcestershire sauce
1 teaspoon garlic powder
$^{1}/_{2}$ teaspoon dry mustard
$^{1}/_{2}$ teaspoon cayenne pepper
$1^{1}/_{2}$ teaspoons kosher salt

1. Preheat the oven to 250°F. Line a baking sheet with parchment paper.

2. Place all the ingredients, except the salt, in a large bowl and toss until the nuts are well coated.

3. Transfer the nuts to the prepared sheet and arrange in a single layer. Place in the oven and cook, stirring every 15 minutes, until the nuts are darkened but not burnt, about 45 minutes.

4. Remove from the oven, immediately loosen the nuts with a metal spatula, sprinkle evenly with the salt, and set aside to cool before serving.

MAKES 2 CUPS

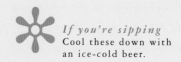

*If you're sipping*
Cool these down with an ice-cold beer.

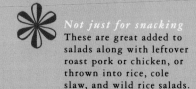

*Not just for snacking*
These are great added to
salads along with leftover
roast pork or chicken, or
thrown into rice, cole
slaw, and wild rice salads.

# bbq pecans

All I can say is, finger-licking good. They remind my friend Susan Benett of Buffalo wings, so whenever I bring them to her house, I always pick up a chunk of hearty blue cheese. These pecans are not for formal dinners; they're for feet-up-on-the-coffee-table afternoons—just add a football game and a beer, or, in Susan's case, an episode of *Iron Chef*.

3 tablespoons unsalted butter, melted, or vegetable oil
2 tablespoons Worcestershire sauce
1 tablespoon ketchup
¼ teaspoon Tabasco sauce
½ teaspoon chili powder
1 teaspoon kosher salt
2 cups raw pecan halves

1. Preheat the oven to 200°F. Line a baking sheet with parchment paper.

2. Place the melted butter, Worcestershire, ketchup, Tabasco, chili powder, and salt in a medium-size bowl and stir to combine. Add the pecans and mix until well coated.

3. Transfer the pecans to the prepared baking sheet and arrange in a single layer. Place in the oven and bake, stirring frequently, until lightly browned, about 30 minutes.

4. Remove from the oven and drain the nuts on paper towels. Serve warm or let cool.

**MAKES 2 CUPS**

# toasted cumin
# hot pecans

**T**his is the quickest and easiest recipe in the book. I love the simplicity and great taste that come from matching the nutty, aromatic cumin with the pecans. The result is a heady, tasty treat just perfect for a late afternoon pick-me-up.

When you are initially toasting the nuts, simply add the cumin seeds about five minutes prior to taking the nuts out of the oven.

2 cups lightly toasted pecan halves (page 12)
1 teaspoon toasted cumin seeds (see headnote)
1 tablespoon extra virgin olive oil
1 teaspoon sweet paprika
½ teaspoon kosher salt
Pinch to ½ teaspoon cayenne pepper, to taste

Place the pecans and cumin with the other ingredients in a medium-size bowl and toss to combine. Serve immediately.

**MAKES 2 CUPS**

*Not just for snacking*
You can also use these to garnish a salad or a soup, especially one with black beans and cilantro.

*If you're sipping*
Sake would be my libation
of choice.

*Not just for snacking*
Include them in sesame
noodles and shredded salads
with chicken, shrimp, or
crabmeat.

# hot pepper
# sesame peanuts

Dark and nutty, toasted sesame oil is pressed from, well, you guessed it: toasted sesame seeds. It is most commonly used in Asian cooking, and once you use it in your cooking, it is hard to go back to the lighter, less fragrant, run-of-the-mill sesame oil. It does need to be used sparingly, as it has the potential to overpower almost any dish.

2 cups lightly toasted shelled peanuts (page 12)
2 teaspoons toasted sesame oil
½ teaspoon garlic powder
½ teaspoon ground ginger
½ teaspoon red pepper flakes
¾ to 1 teaspoon chili powder, to taste
1½ to 2 teaspoons kosher salt, to taste

1. Preheat the oven to 250°F. Line a baking sheet with parchment paper.

2. Place the peanuts, oil, garlic powder, ginger, pepper flakes, and chili powder in a medium-size bowl and toss until the nuts are well coated.

3. Transfer the nuts to the prepared sheet and arrange in a single layer. Place in the oven and bake for 10 minutes.

4. Remove from the oven, immediately loosen the nuts with a metal spatula, sprinkle evenly with the salt, and set aside to cool for 1 hour before serving.

MAKES 2 CUPS

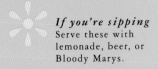

*If you're sipping*
Serve these with
lemonade, beer, or
Bloody Marys.

# salt and chipotle chile almonds

C hipotle chiles are dried, smoked jalapeño peppers. Their rich, sweet-smoky, almost chocolate flavor makes them a welcome addition to almost anything in my house. In fact, there are few foods that my husband doesn't think they improve. Although they are increasingly available in adobo sauce (a dark red chile and vinegar sauce) at grocery stores with good ethnic sections, I have found the ground or crushed form only through Penzeys Spices at www.Penzeys.com or (800) 741-7787.

2 cups raw whole almonds, blanched or skin on
1 teaspoon extra virgin olive oil
1 teaspoon kosher salt
1 teaspoon slightly ground chipotle chile

1. Preheat the oven to 300°F. Line a baking sheet with parchment paper.

2. Place all the ingredients in a medium-size bowl and mix until the nuts are well coated.

3. Transfer the almonds to the prepared sheet and arrange in a single layer. Place in the oven and cook, tossing every 15 minutes, until lightly browned, 40 to 45 minutes.

4. Remove from the oven, immediately loosen the nuts with a metal spatula, and set aside to cool before serving.

MAKES 2 CUPS

# three-pepper almonds

No matter how hard and how often I try, I can't figure out how to get an even, smooth coating on these almonds. The end result is always an almond that is sweet, spicy, and a little gnarly. Serve these with a fresh or dried fruit platter featuring apples, apricots, and plums.

Since Roman times, almonds have been thought to signify five wishes for the bride and groom: health, wealth, happiness, fertility, and longevity. Almonds were once thrown on newlyweds; today, instead, many newlyweds give Jordan almonds to their guests. Pastel-colored, hard candy–coated Jordan almonds are supposed to represent the bitter and the sweet that come with marriage. If you wish for any of the above, try this sweet and spicy recipe instead.

2 teaspoons vegetable oil
2 cups raw whole almonds, blanched or skin on
⅓ cup firmly packed brown sugar
¾ teaspoon red pepper or chipotle flakes
½ teaspoon freshly ground black pepper
½ teaspoon white pepper
1½ teaspoons kosher salt

1. Line a baking sheet with parchment paper.

2. Place a large, heavy-bottomed skillet over medium heat and, when it is hot, add the oil. Add the almonds and cook, stirring, just until they begin to color, about 5 minutes. Add the brown sugar, 1 tablespoon at a time, waiting until each tablespoon melts before adding the next, and cook until all but 1 tablespoon has been added. Sprinkle in the pepper flakes, the black pepper, and the white pepper, stirring all the while.

3. Transfer the almonds to the prepared sheet and sprinkle evenly with the remaining 1 tablespoon brown sugar and the salt. Separate the nuts and set aside to cool before serving.

MAKES 2 CUPS

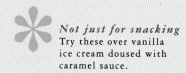

*Not just for snacking*
Try these over vanilla ice cream doused with caramel sauce.

# cumin-cayenne cashews, pine nuts, and pistachios

These are at once buttery, spicy, and peppery. I don't know what it is about this particular combination of flavors—the soft, buttery cashew and the potent, earthy cumin—but these mixed nuts are staggeringly yummy.

If you don't want to use cumin seeds, simply substitute half the amount of ground cumin and add it when you add the salt.

2 tablespoons vegetable oil
2 cups mixed raw cashews, pine nuts, and shelled pistachio nuts
2 teaspoons cumin seeds
1 teaspoon kosher salt
¼ teaspoon cayenne pepper
¼ teaspoon freshly ground black pepper

1. Place a large, heavy-bottomed skillet over medium-high heat and add the oil. When it is very hot, add the nuts. They should sizzle when they hit the oil. Cook, stirring constantly, until they just turn reddish brown, 2 to 3 minutes. Add the cumin seeds and cook until they turn brown, about 30 seconds.

2. Remove the nuts from the skillet with a slotted spoon, transfer to a paper towel to drain, sprinkle evenly with the salt, cayenne, and black pepper, and set aside to cool for at least 1 hour before serving.

MAKES 2 CUPS

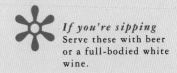

*If you're sipping*
Serve these with beer or a full-bodied white wine.

*If you're sipping*
Don't even think of popping one in your mouth without a beer in your hand. Or at least a glass of milk.

*Not just for snacking*
If you like grinding your own nuts into butter, don't forget these: They make awesome peanut butter. Try Killer Peanuts atop spicy sesame noodles and salads, or chop and mix them into peanut butter cookies or vanilla ice cream.

# killer peanuts

A nd I do mean killer. These are not for shy and retiring types. I'm not even that crazy about peanuts, but I couldn't stop eating these. They are perfect for a big party, accompanied by chips, salsa, and chicken wings.

4 cups lightly toasted shelled peanuts (page 12)
1 tablespoon chile oil (if you want them really hot) or vegetable oil
1 teaspoon red pepper flakes
1 teaspoon sweet or hot paprika
1 teaspoon chili powder
1½ teaspoons kosher salt
½ to 1 teaspoon cayenne pepper, to taste

1. Preheat the oven to 300°F. Line a baking sheet with parchment paper.

2. Place the peanuts and oil in a large bowl and toss to combine. Add the remaining ingredients and toss again to coat evenly.

3. Transfer the nuts to the prepared sheet, place in the oven, and bake for 10 minutes.

4. Remove from the oven, immediately loosen the nuts with a metal spatula, and set aside to cool before serving.

MAKES 4 CUPS

# smoky spicy peanuts

**T**hese are rich, smoky, and, in spite of the lack of sugar, just a little bit sweet.

Liquid smoke is the kind of thing that is easy to disdain if you don't know what it is. The brand I use is Colgin Liquid Smoke, and it's all natural, with no preservatives or additives. According to the company's Web site: "This condensed or 'liquid' smoke is . . . produced by burning fresh cut hickory, mesquite, apple, and pecan wood chips at extremely high temperatures and moisture levels. There's nothing 'synthetic' about it—it's not made from chemicals. It is made by placing high grade smoking woods in sealed retorts, where intense heat makes the wood smolder (not burn), releasing the gases seen in ordinary smoke. These gases are quickly chilled in condensers, which liquefies the smoke; it is then forced through seven refining vats and a large filter, to remove impurities, and finally to the receiving and barreling tanks." The results are—I can't help it—smokin'.

4 cups shelled raw peanuts
2 tablespoons plus 2 teaspoons Worcestershire sauce
2 tablespoons plus 1 teaspoon liquid smoke flavoring
1 tablespoon olive or peanut oil
1 tablespoon plus 1 teaspoon distilled white vinegar
1 tablespoon plus 1 to 2 teaspoons Tabasco sauce, to taste
½ teaspoon cayenne pepper
1 tablespoon plus 1 teaspoon kosher salt

1. Preheat the oven to 250°F. Line a baking sheet with parchment paper.

2. Place all the ingredients, except the salt, in a large bowl and toss until the peanuts are well coated.

3. Transfer the nuts to the prepared sheet and arrange in a single layer. Place in the oven and bake, stirring occasionally, until the nuts turn a deep golden brown, 20 to 30 minutes.

4. Remove from the oven, immediately loosen the nuts with a metal spatula, sprinkle evenly with the salt, and set aside to cool for at least 4 hours and up to overnight.

MAKES 4 CUPS

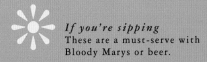

*If you're sipping*
These are a must-serve with Bloody Marys or beer.

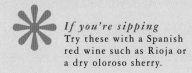

*If you're sipping*
Try these with a Spanish
red wine such as Rioja or
a dry oloroso sherry.

# curried chili cashews

**F**ound in the rainforests, cashews grow at the end of the pear-shaped, astringent-tasting cashew apple. Cashew apples, which are not imported to the United States, are usually left on the tree to rot but are sometimes used for wine, vinegar, juice, and preserves. An entire tree, which can grow up to 40 or 50 feet tall, only produces 10 pounds of nuts per year.

Be patient with these nuts: They are unimpressive just after they get out of the oven. It takes cooling down and sitting—preferably overnight—for the flavors to come through.

1 large egg white (2 tablespoons)
1 teaspoon frozen orange juice concentrate
4 cups raw cashews
¼ cup sugar
1 teaspoon chili powder
½ teaspoon ground cinnamon
½ teaspoon curry powder
1 teaspoon kosher salt

1. Preheat the oven to 225°F. Line a baking sheet with parchment paper.

2. Place the egg white in a stainless steel bowl and whip until it forms soft peaks. Add the orange juice concentrate and whip again. Add the cashews and toss until coated with the mixture. Add the remaining ingredients and toss until the cashews are well coated.

3. Transfer the nuts to the prepared sheet and arrange in a single layer. Place in the oven and bake, stirring every 10 minutes, until browned, 40 to 50 minutes.

4. Remove from the oven, immediately loosen the nuts with a metal spatula, and set aside to cool for at least 1 hour before serving.

MAKES 4 CUPS

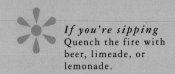

*If you're sipping*
Quench the fire with
beer, limeade, or
lemonade.

# roasted tabasco
# pecans

**H**ot and subtly sweet, these nuts are great with a big hunk of blue cheese. Watch these closely, as Tabasco and Worcestershire sauces burn easily.

1 large egg white (2 tablespoons)
1 tablespoon Tabasco sauce
1 tablespoon light brown sugar
1 teaspoon Worcestershire sauce
½ teaspoon kosher salt, or more to taste
2 cups raw pecan halves

1. Preheat the oven to 250°F. Line a baking sheet with parchment paper.

2. Place the egg white in a large stainless steel bowl and whisk until frothy. Whisk in the Tabasco, brown sugar, Worcestershire, and salt. Add the pecans and toss until completely coated.

3. Transfer the pecans to the prepared sheet and arrange in a single layer. Place in the oven and cook, stirring every 15 minutes, until lightly colored and dried out, about 1 hour and 15 minutes.

4. Remove from the oven, immediately loosen the nuts with a metal spatula, and set aside to cool before serving.

MAKES 2 CUPS

# texas chili–inspired spicy pecans

**V**ery similar in flavor to Texas chili, these crowd pleasers are great to bring to a neighbor's house for an event like the Super Bowl, the Academy Awards, or a holiday party.

2 cups raw pecan halves
2 tablespoons unsalted butter, melted
1 tablespoon sugar
$\frac{1}{2}$ teaspoon ground cumin
$\frac{1}{2}$ teaspoon chili powder
$\frac{1}{4}$ teaspoon red pepper flakes
$\frac{1}{8}$ teaspoon kosher salt

1. Preheat the oven to 325°F. Line a baking sheet with parchment paper.
2. Place the pecans in a large bowl, add the melted butter, and toss until well coated. Place the sugar, spices, and salt in a small bowl, mix well, and sprinkle over the pecans, tossing to coat evenly.
3. Transfer the nuts to the prepared sheet and arrange in a single layer. Place in the oven and bake, stirring occasionally, until lightly browned, 20 to 25 minutes.
4. Remove from the oven, immediately loosen the nuts with a metal spatula, and set aside to cool before serving.

MAKES 2 CUPS

*If you're sipping*
These can accompany almost any beverage, especially beer and soda.

# sweet
## nuts

crunchy chili and brown sugar pecans

paige's snappy toffeed pecans

rum-glazed spiced pecans

indian spiced pecans

sugared bourbon pecans

holy mole pecans

sherry and sugar glazed pecans

charlie's art teacher's orange-cinnamon pecans

jennifer ligeti's classic sugared holiday nuts

jenny's friend leo's grandmother's pumpkin pecans

cinnamon sugar and orange macadamia nuts

rachel travers's cinnamon spiced pecans

honey-cardamom almonds

hot-sweet black and white sesame almonds

paige's cinnamon and clove spiced hazelnuts

lauren's vanilla walnuts

paige's hot peppered candied walnuts

stan frankenthaler's mother's sugar and spice walnuts

coconut curried nuts

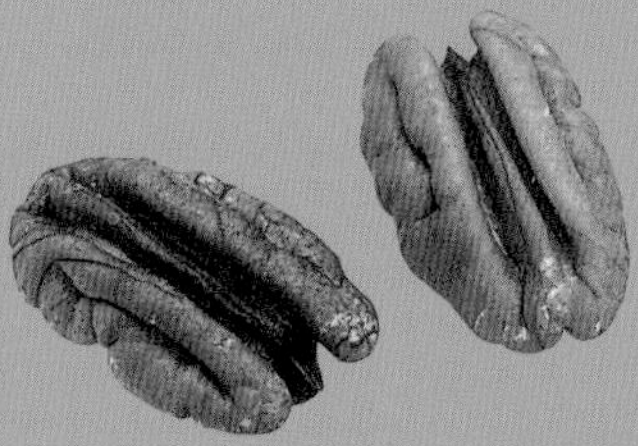

# crunchy chili and brown sugar pecans

Unlike most sweetened pecans, the sugar in these is brown, which results in a nut that is wonderfully crunchy. This recipe is a great vehicle for experimenting with different chili powders.

Include these nuts on a cheese plate with thinly sliced cured meats, berries, and mixed green and black olives.

4 cups raw pecan halves
¼ cup (½ stick) unsalted butter, melted
1 heaping tablespoon chili powder
½ cup firmly packed light brown sugar

1. Preheat the oven to 350°F. Line a baking sheet with parchment paper.
2. Place the pecans and melted butter in a large bowl and toss until the nuts are well coated. Add the chili powder and brown sugar and toss again.
3. Transfer the nuts to the prepared sheet and arrange in a single layer. Place in the oven and bake until the nuts are lightly browned, about 20 minutes.
4. Remove from the oven, immediately loosen the nuts with a metal spatula, and set aside to cool before serving.

MAKES 4 CUPS

*If you're sipping*
Pair these with a fruity white wine such as a New Zealand or Australian Sauvignon Blanc or an Alsatian white.

*Not just for snacking*
Sprinkle on caramelized or grilled onions, or toss into salads with mixed greens and leftover grilled pork or chicken, or, for dessert, mix into vanilla, coffee, or chocolate ice cream. For true decadence, drizzle the ice cream with caramel sauce laced with rum.

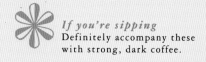

*If you're sipping*
Definitely accompany these
with strong, dark coffee.

*Not just for snacking*
They make a snappy, salty
garnish for crème brûlée or
topping for coffee, caramel,
or chocolate ice cream.

# paige's snappy toffeed pecans

My pal Paige Retus is the brilliant pastry chef at Olives in Boston, and she is incapable of making anything that isn't lip-smacking excellent. She claims that the hard work that goes into making these is well worth the considerable effort, and I couldn't agree more.

1 cup (2 sticks) plus 2 tablespoons unsalted butter
1¾ cups plus 2 tablespoons sugar
1 tablespoon kosher salt
3½ cups raw pecan halves

1. Line a baking sheet with parchment paper.

2. Place the butter in a large, heavy-bottomed skillet over medium-low heat until melted. Add the sugar and salt and stir briskly until the mixture comes together. Add the nuts and cook, stirring evenly and constantly, until the sugar caramelizes and coats the nuts.

3. Cook until the sugar has turned a beautiful oak brown, 5 to 7 minutes, and carefully pour the hot mass onto the prepared sheet. Quickly separate the nuts with forks or tongs. When the nuts have cooled completely, transfer to an airtight container and store for 3 to 5 days or freeze for up to 2 weeks.

MAKES 5 CUPS

# rum-glazed
# spiced pecans

This classic combination of rum and pecans is a winner. Although they taste as if they have taken hours to prepare, they only require a few minutes. Serve these with orange slices.

SPICE MIX
2 tablespoons granulated sugar
1 teaspoon kosher salt
1 teaspoon ground cinnamon
½ teaspoon ground cloves
¼ teaspoon ground allspice

RUM GLAZE
2 tablespoons dark rum
2 teaspoons vanilla extract
1 teaspoon brown sugar
1 teaspoon unsalted butter

2 cups lightly toasted pecan halves (page 12)

1. Line a baking sheet with parchment paper.
2. To make the spice mix, place the spices in a small bowl and mix to combine.
3. To make the glaze, place the glaze ingredients in a medium-size saucepan and bring to a boil over medium heat.
4. Add the pecans to the saucepan and cook until they are well coated and the pan is almost dry, about 1 minute. Spoon the spice mix over the nuts, 1 tablespoon at a time, until they are well coated.
5. Transfer the pecans to the prepared sheet, separate with your hands or a fork, and let sit until completely dried, at least 1 hour and up to overnight.

MAKES 2 CUPS

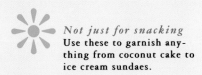

*Not just for snacking*
Use these to garnish anything from coconut cake to ice cream sundaes.

# indian spiced
# pecans

**A** member of the ginger family, cardamom is a warm, sweet-spicy aromatic that can be detected in a lot of Indian and Scandinavian cooking. If you don't have any, simply increase the ground ginger to ¾ teaspoon. Also try this recipe with pistachio nuts.

1 large egg white (2 tablespoons)
¼ cup sugar
1 teaspoon kosher salt
1 teaspoon ground cinnamon
¼ teaspoon ground cardamom
½ teaspoon ground ginger
½ teaspoon dry mustard
2 cups raw pecan halves

1. Preheat the oven to 250°F. Line a baking sheet with parchment paper.

2. Combine all the ingredients, except the pecans, in a large bowl and whisk until well combined. Add the pecans and toss until completely covered with the mixture.

3. Transfer the pecans to the prepared sheet and arrange in a single layer. Place in the oven and cook, stirring every 15 minutes, until lightly colored and dried out, about 45 minutes.

4. Remove from the oven, immediately loosen the nuts with a metal spatula, and set aside to cool before serving.

**MAKES 2 CUPS**

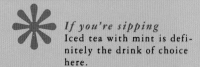

*If you're sipping*
Iced tea with mint is definitely the drink of choice here.

*Not just for snacking*
Add these exotic nuts to basmati rice, rice pudding, or poultry dishes, especially curried chicken salad.

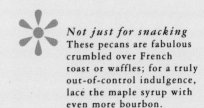

*Not just for snacking*
These pecans are fabulous
crumbled over French
toast or waffles; for a truly
out-of-control indulgence,
lace the maple syrup with
even more bourbon.

# sugared bourbon pecans

I really wasn't too keen on trying a recipe that is essentially boiled nuts in sugar, and yet I found myself unable to resist eating these once they had cooled. My husband, Mark, compares their taste and texture to that of glazed doughnuts, so if you're the type who can't stop at the first doughnut, beware.

1 cup sugar
¼ cup water
6 tablespoons bourbon
¼ teaspoon ground nutmeg
¼ teaspoon ground cinnamon
¼ teaspoon kosher salt
2 cups lightly toasted pecan halves (page 12)

1. Line a baking sheet with parchment paper.

2. Place the sugar, water, bourbon, nutmeg, cinnamon, and salt in a large, heavy-bottomed skillet and bring to a boil over high heat. Cook until the mixture reaches the soft-ball stage, about 235°F on a candy thermometer or when the bubbles have bubbles. Add the pecans and stir until well coated.

3. Transfer the pecans to the prepared sheet, separating the individual nuts, and set aside to cool before serving.

**MAKES 2 CUPS**

*If you're sipping*
Snack on these straight up while
sipping a White Russian or a
coffee liqueur such as Tia Maria.

*Not just for snacking*
Use them to top a hot fudge sun-
dae (coffee, vanilla, chocolate,
butterscotch, and orange are all
good ice cream choices).

# holy mole
# pecans

I totally love these meringue-y, spicy chocolate nuts. Like the Mexican
sauce these are named after, these pecans are rich without being too
sweet.

1 large egg white (2 tablespoons)
1 teaspoon vanilla extract
2 cups raw pecan halves
½ cup sugar
¼ cup cornstarch
1 tablespoon unsweetened cocoa powder
1 teaspoon chili powder
½ teaspoon kosher salt
½ teaspoon ground cinnamon
½ teaspoon ground cumin

1. Preheat the oven to 225°F. Line a baking sheet with parchment paper.
2. Place the egg white in a large stainless steel bowl and whip until
frothy. Whip in the vanilla, then gently add the pecans and toss until completely coated with the mixture.
3. Place the remaining ingredients in a medium-size bowl and toss
until well combined. Add the sugar mixture to the pecans, a quarter of it
at a time, and very gently toss until well coated.
4. Transfer the pecans to the prepared sheet and arrange in a single
layer. Try to not let the pecans touch each other. Place the sheet in the
oven and cook for 30 minutes. Gently turn over the nuts and continue to
cook, stirring every 15 minutes, until the coating is lightly colored and
dried out, about 1 hour and 15 minutes total.
5. Remove from the oven, immediately loosen the nuts with a metal
spatula, and set aside to cool before serving.

**MAKES 2 CUPS**

# sherry and sugar glazed pecans

**D**elicate and sophisticated, these sherried nuts are very adult: a great pre-dinner snack to serve with cheese and other traditional hors d'oeuvres.

1 large egg white (2 tablespoons)
6 tablespoons sherry or champagne
½ to ¾ cup sugar, to taste
1 teaspoon kosher salt
1 teaspoon ground cinnamon
½ teaspoon ground ginger
4 cups raw pecan halves

1. Preheat the oven to 250°F. Line a baking sheet with parchment paper.

2. Place the egg white in a large stainless steel bowl and whisk until frothy. Add the sherry, sugar, and salt and whisk until blended. Add the cinnamon, ginger, and pecans, stirring until well coated.

3. Transfer the pecans to the prepared baking sheet and arrange in a single layer. Place in the oven and cook, stirring every 15 minutes, until they appear dry, about 1 hour and 15 minutes.

4. Remove from the oven, immediately loosen the nuts with a metal spatula, and set aside to cool before serving.

MAKES 4 CUPS

*If you're sipping*
Certainly a good-quality Spanish sherry is the right liquid accompaniment or, if you are using champagne in the nuts, champagne.

*Not just for snacking*
Any leftovers can be added to a composed or lettuce salad.

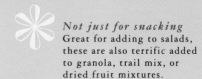

*Not just for snacking*
Great for adding to salads,
these are also terrific added
to granola, trail mix, or
dried fruit mixtures.

# charlie's art teacher's orange-cinnamon pecans

E ight-year-old Charlie Steinberg, the son of our friends Nancy Olin and Steve Steinberg, brought a little cellophane bag of my pecans to his art teacher, who thanked me by offering this recipe.

1 cup lightly toasted pecan halves (page 12)
1 tablespoon frozen orange juice concentrate
$\frac{1}{4}$ teaspoon ground cinnamon
2 tablespoons sugar
$\frac{1}{4}$ teaspoon kosher salt

1. Line a baking sheet with parchment paper.
2. Place all the ingredients in a medium-size bowl and toss until the nuts are well coated.
3. Transfer the nuts to the prepared sheet and arrange in a single layer. Set aside overnight, until the nuts have dried.

MAKES 1 CUP

# jennifer ligeti's classic sugared holiday **nuts**

This is the classic, perfect nut for an open house. My friend Jennifer Ligeti claims that she isn't much of a cook, but every time she gives me a recipe it immediately becomes an essential part of my repertoire. She distributes these in the winter as holiday gifts.

2 large egg whites (¼ cup)
1 cup sugar
½ teaspoon kosher salt
4 cups lightly toasted pecan halves (page 12)

1. Preheat the oven to 250°F. Line a baking sheet with parchment paper.

2. Place the egg whites in a large stainless steel bowl and whisk until frothy. Slowly whisk in the sugar and salt until thick. Fold in the pecans and toss until well coated.

3. Transfer the pecans to the prepared sheet and arrange in a single layer. Place in the oven and bake, stirring gently every 15 minutes, until the meringue covers the nuts with a chewy, pale golden brown coating, 35 to 40 minutes.

4. Remove from the oven and let sit for 5 minutes, then remove the nuts from the pan with a metal spatula and set aside to cool before serving.

MAKES 4 CUPS

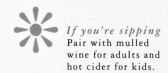

*If you're sipping*
Pair with mulled wine for adults and hot cider for kids.

# jenny's friend leo's grandmother's pumpkin pecans

This is my favorite kind of recipe: one that gets handed down and handed down and, most important, tastes great and works no matter how many adjustments you make to it. When I told Jenny Alperen that I was spending all my time making spiced pecans, she said she had just tasted some that reminded her of pumpkin pie. And then she did the research. Billie Foret, from Pelham, Georgia, gave this recipe to her grandson, Leo Mascotte, who makes them every year for his big Christmas party. I ended up doubling the spices for an even richer flavor.

Allspice, also known as Jamaican pepper, while often thought to be a combination of cinnamon, nutmeg, and cloves, is actually the berry of the evergreen pimiento tree.

1 large egg white (2 tablespoons), lightly beaten
2 tablespoons cold water
½ cup sugar
½ teaspoon kosher salt
¼ teaspoon ground cloves
¼ teaspoon ground allspice
¼ teaspoon ground cinnamon
¼ teaspoon chili powder
¼ teaspoon red pepper flakes
4 cups raw pecan halves

1. Preheat the oven to 250°F. Line a baking sheet with parchment paper.
2. Place the egg white, water, sugar, salt, spices, and pepper flakes in a large bowl and mix well. Let stand for 15 minutes, then add the pecans and toss until well coated.
3. Transfer the pecans to the prepared sheet and arrange in a single layer. Place in the oven and cook, stirring every 15 minutes, until the pecans appear dry, about 1 hour and 15 minutes.
4. Remove from the oven, immediately loosen the nuts with a metal spatula, and set aside to cool before serving.

MAKES 4 CUPS

*If you're sipping*
I like to eat these with hot cider.

*If you're sipping*
These are made even more
indulgent when served
with hot chocolate.

*Not just for snacking*
Crush and add these to
oatmeal cookies.

# cinnamon sugar and orange macadamia nuts

**W**hen we recently received a catalog from a nut roaster, we were amazed to see that the only macadamia offering was roasted and salted. This rendition, reminiscent of the cinnamon sugar toast I lived on as a child, is rich yet delicately flavored.

1 tablespoon unsalted butter, melted
2 cups raw macadamia nuts
1 tablespoon plus 1 teaspoon finely grated orange zest
1 teaspoon ground cinnamon
1 tablespoon plus 1 teaspoon sugar
1 teaspoon kosher salt

1. Preheat the oven to 300°F. Line a baking sheet with parchment paper.

2. Place the melted butter and nuts in a medium-size bowl and toss until well coated. Add the remaining ingredients and mix well to coat evenly.

3. Transfer the nuts to the prepared sheet and arrange in a single layer. Place in the oven and bake until lightly browned, stirring occasionally, 25 to 30 minutes.

4. Remove from the oven, immediately loosen the nuts with a metal spatula, and set aside to cool before serving.

MAKES 2 CUPS

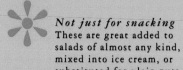

*Not just for snacking*
These are great added to
salads of almost any kind,
mixed into ice cream, or
substituted for plain nuts
in chocolate chip cookies.

# rachel travers's cinnamon spiced pecans

**R**achel is a local food writer who writes frequently for the *Boston Globe*, and both she and her mother, Bernice, have been invaluable sources for countless extraordinary recipes. This combination is, Rachel says, "more complex than you can imagine sugar, salt, and cinnamon to be," and she swears that it's always the most popular item on a buffet table. It can be easily tripled, but if you triple it, only double the egg and water. She also makes this using walnuts.

These are not as sweet as Jennifer Ligeti's pecans (page 73) and are made a bit spicier by the addition of the cinnamon.

1 large egg white (2 tablespoons)
1 teaspoon water
½ cup sugar
1 teaspoon kosher salt
½ teaspoon ground cinnamon
4 cups raw pecan halves

1. Preheat the oven to 225°F. Line a baking sheet with parchment paper.
2. Place the egg white in a large stainless steel bowl and whisk until frothy. Slowly whisk in the water, sugar, salt, and cinnamon until thick. Fold in the pecans and toss until well coated.
3. Transfer the pecans to the prepared sheet and arrange in a single layer. Place in the oven and bake, stirring gently every 15 minutes, until the meringue covers the nuts with a chewy, pale golden brown coating, 35 to 40 minutes.
4. Remove from the oven and let sit for 5 minutes, then remove the nuts from the pan with a metal spatula and set aside to cool before serving.

MAKES 4 CUPS

# honey-cardamom almonds

**W**arm and sweet, cardamom is a member of the ginger family. It is most often tasted in Scandinavian, Middle Eastern, and Indian dishes and smelled in perfumes. Although it is somewhat stronger in seed form, I am a big fan of it ground. Its flavor is definitely prevalent and yet not overpowering in these slightly sticky, slightly peppery, slightly sweet almonds. In fact, it's almost impossible to tell what the spices are. I suggest you leave your guests guessing. Serve these alongside sliced oranges.

    2 tablespoons sugar
    2 teaspoons kosher salt
    1½ to 2 teaspoons ground cardamom, to taste
    ½ teaspoon ground cinnamon
    ½ teaspoon ground ginger
    ¼ cup honey
    2 cups raw whole almonds, blanched or skin on

1. Line a baking sheet with parchment paper.

2. Place the sugar, salt, cardamom, cinnamon, and ginger in a small bowl, mix well, and set aside.

3. Place the honey in a large, heavy-bottomed skillet and bring to a boil over high heat. Add the almonds and cook, stirring all the while, until most of the honey has been absorbed by the almonds and any remaining honey is a deep amber color, 2 to 3 minutes.

4. Remove the almonds from the heat, add a small amount of the sugar mixture to the almonds, and toss. Add the remaining sugar mixture, a little bit at a time, and toss with the almonds until all the mixture has been used.

5. Transfer the almonds to the prepared sheet and arrange in a single layer; separate the almonds with a fork or your hands. Set aside to cool before serving.

MAKES 2 CUPS

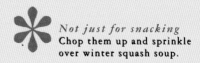

*Not just for snacking*
Chop them up and sprinkle over winter squash soup.

# hot-sweet black and white sesame almonds

**M**y friend Lizzy Shaw, who lives in California and comes to visit once a year, made these last New Year's Eve. When she came back this year, she perfected them. Neither she nor my husband, Mark, could stop eating them.

Although I have used blanched almonds in many of these recipes, I prefer to eat them with the skins on. Some people (not me) consider the skins bitter. If you are one of these people and you like your almonds blanched, simply drop skin-on almonds into a bowl of boiling hot water and let them sit for 2 to 3 minutes. Drain and rub off the skins with your hands. Or you can simply buy them already blanched at the supermarket.

¼ teaspoon ground cumin
1 teaspoon ground ginger
½ teaspoon red pepper flakes
1 tablespoon black sesame seeds
1 tablespoon white sesame seeds
¼ cup plus 2 tablespoons sugar
1½ cups raw whole almonds, blanched, skin on, or a combination

1. Line a baking sheet with parchment paper.

2. In a small bowl, combine the spices, pepper flakes, sesame seeds, and 2 tablespoons of the sugar and mix well. Set aside.

3. Place the remaining ¼ cup of sugar in a large, heavy-bottomed skillet and cook over medium heat until melted, 3 to 4 minutes. Add the almonds and cook, stirring, until they are coated with the sugar syrup.

4. Add a small amount of the sesame seed mixture to the almonds, stirring all the while. Add the remaining mixture, a little bit at a time, and toss until all the mixture has been used.

5. Transfer the nuts to the prepared sheet and arrange in a single layer; separate the almonds with a fork or your hands and set aside to cool before serving.

**MAKES 1½ CUPS**

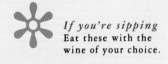

*If you're sipping*
Eat these with the wine of your choice.

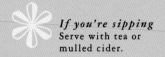

*If you're sipping*
Serve with tea or
mulled cider.

# paige's cinnamon and clove spiced hazelnuts

Hazelnuts, also called filberts or, less frequently, cobnuts, have a crunchy texture. Paige uses these as snacks and dessert garnishes, but I think these sweet and peppery nuts are great to make before prospective buyers come to inspect your house. The aroma will sell even the most rundown shack.

Named after the Latin word for nail, *clavus*, cloves look like little nails (as in hammer, not finger) and although bitter raw, taste warm and slightly sweet when cooked. In most kitchens, whole cloves sit for years and years, losing flavor, waiting to be inserted into a baked ham, their most common ally.

1½ tablespoons sugar
1½ teaspoons ground cinnamon
Pinch of ground cloves
Pinch of kosher salt
1 large egg white (2 tablespoons)
¼ teaspoon vanilla extract
3 cups raw hazelnuts, very coarsely chopped

1. Preheat the oven to 350°F. Line a baking sheet with parchment paper.

2. Place the sugar, cinnamon, cloves, and salt in a medium-size bowl and stir well. Add the egg white and vanilla and gently whisk to combine. Add the nuts and toss to coat thoroughly with the mixture.

3. Transfer the nuts to the prepared sheet and arrange in a single layer. Place in the oven and bake, tossing every 5 minutes, for 15 minutes.

4. Remove from the oven, immediately loosen the nuts with a metal spatula, and set aside to cool before serving.

**MAKES 3 CUPS**

# lauren's vanilla walnuts

The first time that I tested these walnuts, I made a half batch, which my family pretty much devoured. My daughter, Lauren, had earlier begged me to make chocolate chip cookies for her school's Valentine's Day party, but after demolishing these she switched her order to a full batch of nuts. I have no doubt that it was a first for the fourth graders.

I was so excited when I saw vanilla powder, not even knowing what I would do with it. If you can't find it, simply double the amount of vanilla extract, although the vanilla flavor won't be as powerful.

4 cups raw walnut halves
2 tablespoons unsalted butter, melted
6 tablespoons sugar
1 tablespoon vanilla extract
1 tablespoon vanilla powder
1 teaspoon ground cinnamon
1 teaspoon ground nutmeg
1 teaspoon kosher salt
½ teaspoon freshly ground black pepper

1. Preheat the oven to 300°F. Line a baking sheet with parchment paper.

2. Place the walnuts and melted butter in a large bowl and toss until the nuts are well coated. Sprinkle the sugar and vanilla extract over the nuts and toss again until evenly coated.

3. Transfer the walnuts to the prepared sheet and arrange in a single layer. Set aside for 10 minutes.

4. Place the vanilla powder, cinnamon, nutmeg, salt, and pepper in a small bowl, mix well, and set aside.

5. Place the baking sheet in the oven and bake until the nuts are lightly browned, stirring a few times, about 30 minutes.

6. Remove from the oven and immediately loosen the nuts with a metal spatula. While hot, sprinkle the nuts with the spice mix and stir well but gently. Set aside to cool before serving.

MAKES 4 CUPS

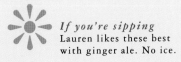

*If you're sipping*
Lauren likes these best with ginger ale. No ice.

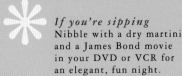

*If you're sipping*
Nibble with a dry martini
and a James Bond movie
in your DVD or VCR for
an elegant, fun night.

# paige's hot
# peppered candied
# walnuts

Although I think of my pal Paige as a brilliant dessert maker, she is more versatile than that. Here she shines with a great cocktail snack, savory and hot and sweet all at the same time.

¾ cup plus 2 tablespoons sugar
2 tablespoons unsalted butter
2 cups raw walnut halves
1 teaspoon kosher salt
½ teaspoon ground cumin
1 teaspoon freshly ground black pepper
¼ teaspoon cayenne pepper

1. Preheat the oven to 350°F. Line a baking sheet with parchment paper.
2. Place ¾ cup of the sugar in a medium, heavy-bottomed skillet and cook over high heat, stirring, until it turns a light caramel color, 4 to 5 minutes. Add the butter and stir until melted. Add the nuts and stir to coat evenly with the mixture.
3. Transfer the nuts to the prepared sheet and arrange in a single layer. Place in the oven and bake, tossing every 5 minutes, until the nuts are toasted, about 15 minutes.
4. Remove from the oven and pour the hot nuts into a medium-size bowl. Add the salt, cumin, black pepper, cayenne pepper, and the remaining 2 tablespoons sugar and very quickly toss the nuts (like flipping pancakes) again and again to coat them evenly.
5. Immediately transfer the nuts to another baking sheet lined with parchment paper and separate the individual nuts with a fork. Allow to cool completely before serving.

MAKES 2 CUPS

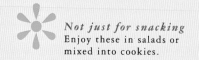

*Not just for snacking*
Enjoy these in salads or
mixed into cookies.

# stan frankenthaler's mother's sugar and spice **walnuts**

Stan's mother was crazy for football. Although she was serious about the professional games on Sunday, she was not a true couch potato; in fact, she spent as much time cooking and greeting guests as she did watching the game. In addition to these sweet and savory nuts, she made little snacks throughout the day, including deviled eggs and quiche.

1 large egg white (2 tablespoons)
2 cups raw walnut or pecan halves, or a combination
6 tablespoons sugar
1 teaspoon kosher salt
1 teaspoon ground ginger
1 teaspoon ground cinnamon
¼ teaspoon ground cloves

1. Preheat the oven to 350°F. Line a baking sheet with parchment paper.

2. Place the egg white in a stainless steel bowl and whip until it forms soft peaks. Add the walnuts and toss until coated. Add the remaining ingredients and toss to coat again.

3. Transfer the nuts to the prepared sheet and arrange in a single layer. Place in the oven and bake, stirring every 10 minutes, until browned, 30 to 40 minutes.

4. Remove from the oven, immediately loosen the nuts with a metal spatula, and set aside to cool before serving.

MAKES 2 CUPS

# coconut curried nuts

Inspired by a recipe in the cookbook *Savor the Moment* by the Junior League of Boca Raton, Florida, this combination is hard to resist: spicy, sweet, and crunchy. You can also make it with any of the nuts alone, rather than in combination.

2 large egg whites (¼ cup)
4 cups mixed raw nuts (including pecans, cashews, almonds, peanuts, and walnuts)
½ cup shredded coconut, sweetened or unsweetened
3 tablespoons sugar
1 tablespoon plus 1 teaspoon curry powder
¼ teaspoon cayenne pepper
1 teaspoon kosher salt
½ teaspoon white pepper

1. Preheat the oven to 225°F. Line a baking sheet with parchment paper.
2. Place the egg whites in a large stainless steel bowl and whip until frothy. Add the nuts and toss until coated. Place the remaining ingredients in another bowl, toss to combine, and add to the nuts. Toss again and coat everything well and evenly.
3. Transfer to the prepared sheet and arrange in a single layer. Place in the oven and cook, stirring every 15 minutes, until lightly colored and dried out, about 1 hour.
4. Remove from the oven, immediately loosen the nuts with a metal spatula, and set aside to cool before serving.

MAKES 4 CUPS

\* *If you're sipping*
These are perfect for munching with red wine, beer, or champagne.

# and two to have fun with

- your basic nut toffee
- your basic nut brittle

# your basic
# nut toffee

**A** candy thermometer is a must! There is no recipe in this book that caused as much frustration and as much revision as this one: I don't even want to describe how sizeable and how icky my failures were. In fact, until I found this recipe, a slight variation of Helen Witty's (from *The Good Stuff Cookbook*), I had despaired of including a recipe for toffee. And yet . . . really good toffee is so good that I persisted.

The amount of nuts in this recipe produces a toffee the way I like it: completely immersed in nuts. If you prefer yours only dotted, simply reduce the quantity of nuts.

If you want your toffee thin, be sure to finely chop the nuts. If you want it thick and bumpy, leave them either whole or coarsely chopped.

¾ cup (1½ sticks) unsalted butter
1¾ cups sugar
2 tablespoons light corn syrup
2 tablespoons cider vinegar
2 cups lightly toasted almonds, pecans, or pistachio nuts (page 12), or the party nuts of your choice (see "Not Your Mother's Peanut Brittle," page 90), chopped or left whole
4 to 6 ounces high-quality semi-sweet, bittersweet, or milk chocolate (optional), to taste, chopped
½ cup finely chopped lightly toasted party nuts of your choice or coconut (optional)

1. Line a baking sheet with parchment paper. Butter an offset spatula.
2. Place the butter in a large, heavy-bottomed saucepan (larger than you imagine you will need) and, when it is halfway melted, add the sugar, corn syrup, and vinegar. Bring to a boil over high heat and continue to cook, stirring the whole time, until it reaches the soft-crack stage and is a pale golden brown, 275° to 290°F on the candy thermometer, 12 to 15 minutes.
3. Quickly stir in the nuts and pour immediately onto the prepared sheet. Using the buttered spatula, spread the toffee as thinly as possible.

Let stand for 1 minute, then sprinkle with the chopped chocolate, if using. Let stand for 2 minutes to soften, then spread the chocolate with the back of a spoon or a rubber spatula until it has melted. Sprinkle evenly with the chopped nuts. (Omit them if you aren't using the chocolate.) Set aside to cool completely, then break into large pieces.

4. Store the toffee in an airtight container, where it will keep for 2 to 3 weeks.

**MAKES ABOUT 1 POUND**

# NOT YOUR MOTHER'S PEANUT BRITTLE

I initially made toffee and brittle as a vehicle for using the broken bits of pecans that I felt were too small to bag and sell. Although these two recipes are great using the nuts I have specified, they are really special—in fact sublime—when made with nuts that have already been flavored. Any of these *Party Nuts!* recipes are great in brittle and toffee; the spicy ones are my favorites.

# your basic
# nut brittle

Although I am specific in my instructions below as to how far to cook the sugar, I always go just beyond that, to almost burning it. Well, the truth is, as you can imagine, that it started out as a mistake but now I do it on purpose: I love the resulting caramel-y, almost chocolatey taste.

1 cup sugar
½ cup water
1½ to 2 cups lightly toasted almonds, pecans, or pistachio nuts
(page 12), or the party nuts of your choice (see "Not Your Mother's
Peanut Brittle," left), chopped or left whole

1. Line a baking sheet with parchment paper. Butter an offset spatula.
2. Place the sugar and water in a large, heavy-bottomed saucepan (larger than you imagine you will need), bring to a boil over high heat, and continue to boil until the sugar has dissolved, about 5 minutes. Reduce the heat to medium and simmer until it reaches the hard-crack stage and is cinnamon colored, 300°F on a candy thermometer, 12 to 15 minutes.
3. Quickly stir in the nuts and pour immediately onto the prepared sheet. Using the buttered spatula, spread the brittle as thinly as possible. Set aside to cool completely, then break into large pieces.
4. Store the brittle in an airtight container, where it will keep for 2 to 3 weeks.

MAKES ABOUT ⅔ POUND

# index

# about the author

Sally Sampson is a senior writer at *Cooks Illustrated*. Her work has appeared in *Bon Appétit, Food & Wine,* and the *Boston Globe,* among other publications. She is the author of *The Bake Sale Cookbook* and *The $50 Dinner Party* and the co-author of six cookbooks. Sampson's Nuts (877-977-0077) can be found in specialty stores around Boston, where she lives.